WEALTH C

WEALTH OF COLONIES

BY

W. K. HANCOCK

THE MARSHALL LECTURES
delivered at Cambridge
on 17 and 24 February 1950

CAMBRIDGE
AT THE UNIVERSITY PRESS
1950

CAMBRIDGE UNIVERSITY PRESS
Cambridge, New York, Melbourne, Madrid, Cape Town,
Singapore, São Paulo, Delhi, Tokyo, Mexico City

Cambridge University Press
The Edinburgh Building, Cambridge CB2 8RU, UK

Published in the United States of America by Cambridge University Press, New York

www.cambridge.org
Information on this title: www.cambridge.org/9781107681774

First published 1950
First paperback edition 2011

A catalogue record for this publication is available from the British Library

ISBN 978-1-107-68177-4 Paperback

PREFACE

THESE LECTURES are printed as they were delivered except that some figures have been brought up to date. The title also has been changed; but even so, it does not completely fit the subject matter, which includes some discussion of President Truman's Fourth Point and the problems of 'under-developed countries' in general. Not all these countries are 'colonial' in the political sense. Some of the poorest of them possess the trappings of sovereignty: conversely, some non-sovereign territories have developed their resources with great rapidity. The experience of the British Commonwealth suggests that economic and political dependence are matters of degree and that advancement or stagnation is to be explained by the interaction of economic, social and political influences. The first lecture attempts to bring this complicated process into focus. The second lecture reviews current problems of development and welfare within the British Commonwealth.

W.K.H.

JULY
1950

WEALTH OF COLONIES

I

I AM HERE by the particular kindness of your Faculty, a grateful Marshall Lecturer, if an unlikely one. You are economists, I am an historian: in billing myself to lecture on the Political Economy of Colonies, I should have added—'as an historian sees it'. And even then I should have defined my intention a bit more strictly. After nearly ten years of absence from colonial studies, I am looking for my compass bearings again; the development policies of to-day are new to me and I want to get them into focus. But this attempt must wait until my next lecture: I have to re-discover old landmarks in the past before I start dotting the present and the future with new ones.

Are landmarks any use at all in a thick fog? Our generation has befogged itself by its inveterate and atrocious abuse of language. There is no stability in the words we use; they change their meaning and emotional tone from country to country, from decade to decade, from person to person; the same word is to one man a term of scientific description, to another a war-cry, to a third an incantation. Consider the word *colony;* in my habit of speech, any political dependency is a colony; but Americans commonly employ a double standard of language: their own political dependencies are territories—a worthy name; but ours are colonies—a word of shame. To the Russians, the word is a missile of political warfare. Meanwhile, the plodding English retain it for simple description. Unfortunately, the things described do not stand still: in my own lifetime, the peoples of *Magna Britannia*[1] have moved from dependent to sovereign status: when now we speak of colonies we envisage indigenous populations within the tropics, not emigrant communities of European stock. Yet I like to recall that the Hancocks of Massachusetts were colonials, and so were the Hancocks of Australia.[2]

Still more confusing is the word *imperialism.* Muddle-headed historians in Great Britain and America use this word with Heaven-knows how many shades of meaning, while Soviet writers are using it to summarise a theory and wage a war.

[1] This phrase echoes *Magna Graecia* and thereby connotes 'colonies of settlement'.

[2] I myself was born a colonial—just in time, for on the first day of this century my colony, Victoria, became a State of the Commonwealth of Australia. I suppose I became a dominional then—and now, under our new-fangled laws of nationality, my only chance of recovering my original status is to apply for United Kingdom citizenship which carries with it citizenship in the colonies.

Communists did not invent it; as Professor Koebner has recently reminded us,[1] it came into existence about one-hundred years ago, when apprehensive and scandalised Liberals hurled it against Napoleon III. Since then it has had many connotations and has many times changed its tone. There have been times and places where it has enjoyed a fleeting prestige; but throughout the longer part of its short life, and most certainly in our own generation, it has remained what it was at the beginning, a missile of political warfare. Lenin certainly used it that way. He hurled it with gusto at those unblushing, impotent, insincere, dishonest, cynical, opportunist, vulgar persons who did not think like Lenin. I have culled the adjectives—they are but a selection—from Lenin's own book.[2] They hardly suggest the dispassionate attitude of science. Yet Lenin believed himself to be a social scientist. To him, imperialism was a scientific concept—a master concept indeed; for it contained the explanation of a decisive chapter in human history.

Lenin discusses a process of industrial change. Units of industrial production are growing in size and combining with each other in trusts and cartels:

[1] 'The Concept of Economic Imperialism', by R. Koebner, in *Economic History Review*, Second Series, Vol. II, No. 1.

[2] *Imperialism the Highest Stage of Capitalism*, written at Zurich in the spring of 1916, translated into English 1920 (The Little Lenin Library, Martin Lawrence Ltd.).

9

a new capitalism is thus arising, monopoly capitalism. (He chooses a word reverberant with the indignation of three centuries.) The same process of concentration has been taking place in finance; the banks have amalgamated and have made themselves masters of the capital that the industrialists use: consequently, monopoly capitalism is also finance capitalism. (He borrows a phrase from the Austrian Hilferding.) This monopoly-finance-capitalism is aggressively expansionist. Its typical export is capital itself, in contrast with the goods that were the exports of capitalism in its earlier, competitive stage. What are its consequences? One consequence is the exploitation of colonial peoples; it subjects them to the capitalist law of increasing misery and destroys their liberty. Another consequence is war. Markets are partitioned among the great capitalist combines; territories are partitioned and re-partitioned among the Great Powers; economic conflict erupts in war. Capitalism blows itself up. The new order of social production bursts from the shell of private appropriation within which it has been fashioned. Imperialism, capitalism's highest stage, is also its death struggle.

I personally have little confidence in a narrator of social change who chooses abstract words as his *dramatis personae;* but I have faithfully reported Lenin's argument. In criticising it, I feel some compunction. Lenin's stature among men of action is very great. Considered as action, his book *Imperialism* makes sense. But I have to ask whether it makes logical and historical sense.

I begin by approving Lenin's attempt to tie together the logical and chronological strands of his argument. I accept his contention that it is futile to explore historical causes and effects except within a framework of time. In the age of great industrial and financial combinations, the contact of peoples and the conflicts of classes and states have obviously a different meaning from the one they had in the age when industrial units were numerous, moderate in size and competitive. So far I go with Lenin: I part company with him only when he asserts that the new meaning is the whole meaning—for example, that monopoly capitalism is nowadays the sole or the sufficient explanation of a Franco-German struggle for the possession of Lorraine. It seems to me one thing to examine historical events within their immediate framework of time and quite another thing to make each slab of time completely self-contained and separate from its predecessors. But this is by the way: what really interests me is Lenin's manner of manoeuvre within the chronology of his own choice. He was faced with a dilemma. When he was discussing economic institutions, he had to choose a late opening date for the period of imperialism, for he could not put the dominance of industrial combinations earlier than the first decade of the twentieth century, and even this was too early for Great Britain, which, after all, possessed the largest empire in the world.[1] But he had to choose an early opening date for the imperialist period when he was discussing the alleged political consequences of industrial and financial trustification; everybody knew, for example, that the partitioning of the New World was practically completed before the nineteenth century closed. Can the political consequences of an economic process precede the process itself? Lenin sought to escape his dilemma by shuffling his chronological cards; he produced the early date or the late one in different parts of his book to suit the changing needs of his argument. Perhaps it is naïve of me to explain this confusion by a crack in his logic; it may be merely a crack in his honesty.

I see in his exposition a second crack which he tries to cover by bluster. The luckless Karl Kautsky had envisaged a new order of *ultra-imperialism*—an internationalisation of political institutions which would reflect the economic internationalisation achieved by interlocking monopolies. Kautsky's prognostication was unplausible in fact; but was it so unplausible in Marxist theory? Lenin called Kautsky a fool because he did not see that the partitioning of markets is proportionate to power.

[1] Finance Capitalism, as Lenin defines it, did not at any time establish itself in Great Britain.

12

What kind of power? The power of sovereign states and the economies which take shape within their framework. Here Lenin smuggles in a political factor which governs economic evolution, and is not merely governed by it. In doing so, he contradicts his oft repeated assertion that monopoly capitalism by itself governs the politics of the imperialist stage no less than its economics. The contradiction does credit to his realism, for he would not have been a successful revolutionary had he not been a Machiavellian as well as a Marxist. The luckless Kautsky threatened to give the game away by sticking woodenly to Marxist rules. No wonder Lenin blustered.

I know that you have in Cambridge ardent Leninists who may want to argue with me on these points of theory; but I must now pass on to my more important task of confronting Lenin's theory, such as it is, with some historical facts. In his sketch of the trend towards industrial aggregation and combination there is much truth; but in other parts of his book there is much error. In particular, his argument at two crucial stages transgresses the limits of pardonable inaccuracy.

I shall mention first his treatment of the relation between private overseas investment and the rivalries of the Great Powers. He argued that it was the investing capitalists who pushed their governments into dangerous diplomatic adventures and he asserted that this was the root cause of war in the imperialist age; but Professor Staley's case studies have proved the very opposite. More frequently it was the politicians and the military men who pushed the investors into dangerous adventures. Financiers may have given the British Government a powerful push towards the South African war; but the Italian and Russian governments pushed their financiers into situations portending war against Turkey and Japan. Moreover, Russia and Italy were both net importers of capital, not exporters of it as expansionist States ought to be—if they behaved by the book. The Swiss, on the other hand, surpassed all other nations in their holdings of foreign investments per head of population; but Switzerland was not an expansionist power. What about Great Britain? Sometimes she seems to behave by the book and sometimes not. All through the nineteenth century she had been extending her overseas possessions and all through the century her capitalists—though as producers they were still fiercely competitive—had been investing money overseas. By 1855, they had £450 millions invested abroad; by 1870, £1,000 millions; by 1885, £1,600 millions; by 1900, £2,000 millions. This long-continuing correlation between overseas investment and territorial expansion might have been grist to Lenin's mill if he had not made such a fetish of the novelty of his own imperialist process. He said flatly that the export of capital did not 'develop formid-

able proportions until the beginning of the twentieth century'. He also asserted that the greater part
of British capital was invested in British colonies. If
he had taken the trouble to consult Sir George Paish's
analysis, he would have found out that the facts were
otherwise. But he did not really care for facts.

There is in the book a second factual blunder
which I must briefly discuss. Lenin contends that
impoverishment and servitude accompany capital
when it is sent abroad. Sometimes, as I shall show
later on, they may do so; but can we accept the
statement that they do so as a general rule? I should
like to hear the comments on it of Professor Louis
Hacker, the historian of American capitalism who
has recently recalled the services of British investors
to the United States;[1] they financed the railways and
before that the canals and earlier still the Louisiana
Purchase; at one crucial stage after another they
played their essential part in that drama of the expanding frontier which many historians have
presented as an all-American epic. What happened
in America has happened in many other places; as
an Australian I learned long ago that it is sound
policy for an under-developed country to borrow
at five per cent in order to earn seven per cent. But
the refutation of Lenin need not depend on selected
histories. Professor Staley has given dollar figures
per head of population for the foreign debts of the

[1] *England and America*, by Louis Hacker (O.U.P. 1949).

capital importing countries in the years 1930-1.[1] At the head of the list stand three sovereign States of the British Commonwealth: Canada, $623 per head of population; Australia, $592; New Zealand, $555. These three countries are not notorious for their poverty! If you are looking for real poverty, you must go to the countries whose capital imports per head of population have been low—to Haiti, where Staley's figure is $11, to British West Africa, where it is $10; to India, where it is $8; to China, where it is $7. I am not suggesting that the poverty of these countries can be cured by immense doses of foreign capital, or that, even if it could be so cured, sufficient capital would be forthcoming. The problems of development and welfare are more complicated than that: there is scarcity of resources on the supply side and on the demand side a medley of circumstances which determine the credit-worthiness and absorptive capacity of would-be borrowers—their natural resources, their market opportunities, their population trends, their habits of labour, enterprise and saving, their systems of family and kinship, their religious beliefs, their political capacities—a score of factors which found no place in Lenin's philosophy. I shall discuss some of these factors later on. Meanwhile, let us simply take note that the correlation

[1] *War and the Private Investor*, by Eugene Staley (New York 1935), p. 14. The figures are quoted from the *Statistical Handbook of the League of Nations*, 1930-1, pp. 18-25.

between capital movements and poverty appears generally to be the very reverse of the one Lenin pretended to discover.

And let us at last take leave of *imperialism*. It is a pseudo-concept which sets out to make everything clear and ends by making everything muddled; it is a word for the illiterates of social science, the callow and the shallow who attempt to solve problems without mastering a technique.

Another blessed word, *trusteeship*, now stands in my path. It is not a word of sweeping intellectual pretension but one of high moral profession; its connotations are ethical and political. Nevertheless, it has always readily associated itself with those concepts of economic policy that are from time to time in fashion. In recent years, at Lake Success, orators in the Trusteeship Council and the Fourth Committee of the Assembly have been asking questions like these: Why are wages so much lower in the Belgian Congo than they are in Brussels? Why is there not a school for each five hundred children of the Belgian Congo and eight teachers to each school? Why is there no University for the Trusteeship Territories of Africa? Why are there no heavy industries? Why is the tribal system still maintained? . . . We should be naïve indeed if we imagined that these questions are asked with a simple zeal to elicit truth;[1]

[1] Some of the orators represent sovereign States whose standards of welfare compare ill with those of adjacent colonies. More than half the

B

but they do at least reveal the line of propaganda that suits present times. All of them assume that governments have a direct obligation to promote economic development and social welfare in the colonial territories under their rule. Trusteeship nowadays must express itself in the idiom of economic planning and the welfare state.

It was not ever thus. Throughout the nineteenth century the apostles of trusteeship insisted that governments would best fulfil their obligations to colonial peoples, not by extending their economic functions but by contracting them. We can symbolise British colonial policy[1] in this period as an alliance between Wilberforce and Adam Smith. These two men, in their separate ways, affirmed

members of U.N.O. have in distant or recent years achieved sovereignty by separating from the Spanish, or the Turkish, or the British or some other Empire: the politicians of these States tend to be committed at home and abroad to an anti-imperial attitude. Meanwhile, the States of the Soviet *bloc* are waging political warfare against the West. We shall not be surprised that they have found good opportunities at Lake Success if we recall that the Trusteeships of U.N.O. belong to a wider category of international instruments—trusteeships, mandates, condominions, capitulations, minority treaties—phenomena which commonly appear in faults or fissures where the crust of the world's peace has cracked, or threatens to crack. Along these fissures, sovereignty is in greater or less degree ambiguous because the conflicting powers have been unwilling to see it pass *in toto* to their rivals or potential rivals: in default of a united Concert of Powers, the areas of ambiguous sovereignty naturally remain—what they were originally—areas of international dissension. *See H. H. Duncan Hall—Mandates Dependencies and Trusteeship,* (Carnegie Endowment 1948) Ch.1.

[1] Not of course the whole of it: there is for example the Edward Gibbon Wakefield strand of policy.

both the value of the individual and the unity of humanity. Wilberforce, the religious preacher, derived these principles from the universal father-hood of God; Smith, the philosopher and economist of natural law, derived them from 'the natural propensity of mankind'. One man took it for granted that any individual of any race would find a fuller life within the expanding Christian Church; the other took it for granted that he would live more abundantly within the expanding economy of Europe. Both men discovered in society, not in the State, the principle of healthy growth. Christianity and commerce were the true creators of liberty and welfare; the State was, at best, the hinderer of hindrances. In the administration of dependencies its function was to maintain a respectable code of conduct to which individuals of all races must con-form; in particular, it must defend indigenous peoples against the aggressions of ruthless Europeans. This the British State had begun to attempt well before the close of the eighteenth century. Settlers in America were overflowing into the hunting lands of the western tribes; a royal proclamation in 1763 sought to restrain them. Traders in India were abusing their mixed powers of commercial mono-poly and political sovereignty; Parliament circum-scribed and in the end abolished these powers. Planters in the West Indies had built a great industry upon slavery. Parliament abolished the slave trade and slavery itself. The spirit which informed these acts expressed itself, for more than a century and in many parts of the world, in a continuing policy. Sometimes the policy was successful and sometimes not; but its purpose was always clear—to establish a just order which would defend the weaker peoples until they were able to meet the stronger upon equal terms. How would this come about? Most progressive people in the nineteenth century believed that it would come about without direct action by the State in the economic sphere: the 'natural and free' operation of economic and social laws would do the job. So the imperial trustee left education to the missionaries and trade to the traders.

The traders and the missionaries were not only British subjects but also foreigners. The British state, by retreating from the wide province of economic and social action into the citadel of law and order, left the doors of its dependencies open to enterprising people of all nations. This retreat of the State led by degrees to the policy of Dual Mandate which was still very much with us in the early decades of this century. It was a policy that seemed to offer an harmonious and enduring solution of those problems that are most vexing and dangerous to an imperial power. As trustee for the commerce of the world— so Sir Eyre Crowe argued in a famous memorandum —a free trading Britain offered equality to the traders, migrants and investors of all nations and thereby assuaged foreign jealousy of her great possessions. As trustee for peoples unable as yet to stand fully upon their own feet in the modern world, she offered cheap imports and a world market for exports—the same boons as had enabled America and many other new countries to follow the path of economic opportunity.

The beam of light that Adam Smith had thrown upon the American colonies illuminated a century and more of British theory and practice. By his teaching, it was the law of comparative costs, operating outside political sovereignty and sometimes in defiance of it, that explained the dazzling American prosperity: other dependencies would prosper comparably if only the imperial state would bow itself out from its rôle of economic regulator and allow the political economy of colonies to lose itself in non-political, international economics. I want to test this hypothesis by some historical examples and I shall begin with one that illustrates its strength: I take it from Mr R. M. Hartwell's[1] unpublished study of Tasmanian history from 1820 to 1850—a trivial history in its scale, but not in its significance. We see in 1820 a population of five and a half thousand people of whom more than half are convicts; in 1850 we see—despite the convict flood that

[1] It is a thesis in the library of Sydney University: I am grateful to the author for permitting me to use it here. I hope it may be revised for publication.

drenched Tasmania throughout these thirty years—
a population of sixty thousand, of whom more than
two thirds are free. At the beginning of the story
we see a parasitic and immobile prison farm; at the
end we see a dynamic economy—a wide diversity of
primary and secondary employments, credit worthi-
ness to procure capital from outside, thrift and
intelligence to accumulate and invest it domestically,
a class of resourceful risk takers and managers, a
mobile and adaptable labour force. In this brief
period of thirty years the seeds of freedom, rooting
themselves at first in cracks and crannies of the prison
wall, have sprouted and grown until the wall has
been destroyed and freedom everywhere sets the
tone and makes the pace of life. I have no time to
review the story in detail but I shall show you some
flashes of it. In the beginning, Tasmania produces
no exchangeable wealth of any kind; what it contains is inert nature and a few thousands of primitive
food-gathering aborigines. The convicts and their
jailers arrive. The government is the only entre-
preneur and its commissariat expenditure—merely
to keep its subjects alive— is at first the only form of
investment. But soon the government finds itself
compelled to delegate economic functions; it leases
land—later it sells its—to military officers or civilian
officials or emancipated convicts; in time, a trickle
of free immigrants arrive to take up land. The
government delegates its trading powers; a clique

22

of merchants profit and profiteer by handling the import trade; soon they begin to look about for exports. Seals abound on Tasmania's rocky coasts; black whales are plentiful in the estuaries and bays. In the pupping season the seals are an easy prey; the mothers are killed and their young left to die. By the end of the 1830's the sealers have exterminated the sealing industry. By the end of the 1840's the whalers have exterminated the whaling industry. But the merchants have taken good profits from both industries and have accumulated investible capital. Meanwhile, opportunities have been expanding on the land; by the 1820's it produces more than enough meat for home consumption; the sheep owners have begun to breed their flocks and manage their pastures with an eye upon Yorkshire's demand for wool. In quantity and quality of pastoral land, Tasmania falls far short of New South Wales, but she finds compensations; New South Wales is an importer of food and offers market opportunity to Tasmanian growers of wheat and other crops. The primary industries build firm foundations for an expanding economy. Secondary industries soon arise. As the population grows and becomes more diverse consumer needs increase; market opportunity offers itself to millers and brewers and distillers, to soap-boilers and candle-makers, to smiths and saddlers and hatters and other small manufacturers. On Tasmania's well-wooded estuaries a large industry arises; by the 1840's, the yards of Hobart are building sailing-ships up to six hundred tons and producing a larger mercantile tonnage than all the rest of Australia. The shipbuilding industry employs directly a sizeable labour force and considerable capitals, and it has called into existence associated industries such as cooperage, block making, sail making, saw milling. In these ways, manufacture grows up alongside agriculture. Meanwhile, Tasmania has equipped itself with the financial institutions appropriate to its growing and thriving production.

In most of this progress merchant capitalists have been the driving force. Their accounts and letter books, some of which survive, bear the stamp of men who ardently pursue their own interest. Are not these men led by an invisible hand to pursue at the same time the community's interest? In thirty years they have led Tasmanian society out of the house of bondage. Tasmania in 1850 is earning her own keep, making her own fortune, working her way towards economic and political self determination. The magic of the market and the law of comparative costs are performing once again the miracle that Adam Smith had acclaimed in colonial America. What a success story! Can you find in Samuel Smiles anything to beat it? ... But perhaps you remember what I said about the seals and the whales and you may want to ask me what happened to the aborigines. I shall have to answer this question later on—and perhaps some others that you have in mind.

In my second short story, deliverance out of the house of bondage is again the theme. This time we find ourselves in eighteenth century Liverpool, in the forts and hulks of the West African coast, in the slave ships making their 'middle passage' to the American plantations. The slave trade was a strong vested interest which British business men, economists and statesmen of the eighteenth century believed to be 'very profitable to the nation in general'; but in 1807 Parliament abolished it. We usually proclaim abolition as a triumph of 'the saints' over the sinners,—but this oversimplifies the issue and takes away some of its interest. Many writers have praised the virtue of Wilberforce and his friends; I shall praise their commonsense. Moral reform was their *métier;* but I doubt whether they rated so high as our age does the efficacy of undiluted moral exhortation. They appealed both to principle and to profit; they invited traders to establish 'a just and equitable traffic' in the products of African labour, in place of the unjust traffic in human lives. They summoned the Royal Navy to police the West African coast and their successors summoned British military power to pacify the hinterland. The experience of West Africa from the beginning of the nineteenth century to its end proved their judgement right: a 'just and equitable commerce' could not strike firm roots except within the shelter of a *pax*. Even within that shelter it could not multiply and fructify unless it were watered by the inclination both of Europeans and Africans to better their private conditions. I cannot think it a misfortune for Africa[1] that the Christian moralists of that time had learned their economics from Adam Smith. I do not see how abolition could have been brought about in 1807 had not Liverpool been finding alternative employment in the new and thriving cotton trade. Nor do I see how West African society could even have begun to lift itself out of its misery had not the growing populations of the new industrial cities of Britain and Europe demanded soap, candles, and margarine. Traders and peasants in the palm country of the West coast went into business to satisfy this demand. The oil and kernel trades fluctuated throughout the nineteenth century and their trends of growth were often unspectacular; but they did nevertheless lay permanent foundations for economic progress in West Africa. A dramatic quickening of the rhythm of progress occurred towards the end of the century. Old markets boomed; new markets opened in bewildering succession for cocoa, cotton, groundnuts, gold, tin and other products. The growth of export trade stimulated the division of labour in village and town and promoted the growth

[1] The West Indies, however, are a different story.

of local trade. In some districts, most notably the cocoa growing ones, there occurred a sensational expansion of private incomes. Public revenue grew and with it the capacity to borrow money abroad. The governments realised that the further expansion of private business and taxable wealth depended upon their own willingness to supply public works and services. And so we approach—not so suddenly nor so recently as is sometimes suggested—the development and welfare programmes of our own generation.

Is the history of British West Africa another success story? When I remind myself that the illicit slave trade dominated the coast up to the eighteen sixties and that slave raiding afflicted the northern interior almost to the end of the century, I think it is. I am sure it must have seemed so to the men who saw the first railway train steam into Kano just before the first World War. But we, since then, have had so many years of war, inflation, boom, depression, inflation once again—we are still in the middle of all this and are not yet sure of the outcome. Meanwhile, we have acquired new concepts of economic and social change and new techniques for investigating it. To us its processes seem far more complicated and disturbing than they seemed a few generations ago to the apostles of Christianity and commerce. Were I now to look back again upon the story I have just told, I could show that it has sombre threads which Adam Smith's lamp cannot reveal—the loss of old securities, the growth of new inequalities, above all the spiritual bewilderment that is so brilliantly depicted in Joyce Carey's *Mister Johnson*.

I shall now explore these themes in the history of Burma under British rule. My guide, Mr J. S. Furnival,[1] permits me to begin on the note of liberal optimism, though for my ending he demands a different note. Burma, when she was taken by successive stages during the nineteenth century into the British Empire, enjoyed a classical plenty of cheap land but did not suffer from the extreme poverty of labour which elsewhere had to be made good by immigration; moreover, the Burmans had never shown signs of incapacity to use their rich natural resources intelligently. It was therefore to be expected, by the rules of political economy, that enlarged market opportunities would yield their natural fruit in an enhancement of Burmese wealth and welfare. The British conquerors respected the rules of political economy: in contrast with Dutch practice in Java, they established in Burma a free and equal trade under direct administration and the rule of law. This seemed to suit the Burmans, who brought their teak and rice to market, spent their money as they chose, and found themselves, Mr Furnival believes, both wealthier and happier than they had been before.

[1] *Colonial Policy and Practice*, by J. S. Furnival (C.U.P. 1948).

But this was only the first stage of Burma's contact with the western economy. Mr Furnival believes that things went badly wrong in the later stages. He takes 1870, the year when the Suez Canal was opened, as the hinge of Burma's modern economic history. I myself think that railway building in India and the growth of population and markets there may have had more practical effect upon Burma than the opening of the Canal; be this as it may, 1870 marks well enough the beginning of Burma's decisive incorporation within the world economy. Should not the Burmans have profited, as their trading partners did, from the expansion of international markets? This was the period in which the sparsely populated delta of the Irrawaddy was transformed into a great factory for producing rice. Even so, there was no pressure of population upon the land; as the total area of cultivation increased, so also did the average size of the peasant holding; the output of rice per man rose as the volume of exports rose. Yet there was no exaggerated dependence on rice as a cash crop; the peasant produced food for his family as well as food for sale. Moreover, the terms of trade were good: from the 1870's to the 1920's there was a general upward trend in the price of rice and a downward trend in the price of cotton goods; the peasant was not only producing on the average more units of rice but buying with each unit more of the things he needed. Despite all this, Mr Furnival believes that his condition was growing all the time steadily worse.

He finds the explanation not in the economic process itself but in the social changes that accompanied the economic process. Plenty of cheap land has been a trap for the Burmese peasant. He seeks to acquire more land than he can equip; he borrows money from the gombeen man and finds within a few years that he must surrender his land to clear his debt. Peasant ownership nowadays is an illusion; peasants are 'tenants one day, labourers the next'; to the enquirer who looks below legal forms, the rice lands of Lower Burma offer a spectacle of ever changing occupancy and camouflaged absentee ownership. Certainly the world market for rice has brought prosperity into Lower Burma; but it has brought it into the towns and particularly into the houses of the Chettyar money lenders, not into the peasant huts of the Irrawaddy delta.

Up to 1870 or thereabouts the cultivators had not only retained the profit of their holdings but had also supplemented their incomes as cultivators by bye-employments such as fishing, fish curing, boat building and weaving. But, from the 1870's onwards, imported products and methods progressively ousted the traditional home-produced goods and services. This change illustrates the familiar principle of the survival of the cheapest which economists have been wont to acclaim as a condition of economic progress; if things go as they should, the labour released from time-consuming employments will find more profitable alternative employments. In Burma, however, the new avenues of employment were for the most part filled not by displaced Burmans but by immigrants —by Europeans in the higher grades and by Indians both in the lowest grades and in the middle ones.

From the very beginning, European business had come to Burma not only with the capital it needed but with the management; in consequence, the great capitalist enterprises of today—timber mills, river transport, ruby mines, oil fields—are from the Burman point of view 'foreign' and a target for a nationalist attack. In addition, European business, from the beginning right up to recent time, has imported a good part of the labour it has needed. We have seen that the Burmans responded quickly enough to some kinds of economic demand; but there were certain employments they were slow to enter. When, for example, the Government of Arakan wished in the '30's and '40's of the last century to build roads, it found Burmese labour scarce and dear, so it sent to India first for convicts, later for coolies. It sent again to India when it needed policemen and clerks and hospital attendants. The business firms sent to India for shop assistants, book-keepers and technicians. It was cheaper, Mr

Furnival observes, to import Indians than to train Burmans. Thus, not only the lowlier employments became predominantly foreign but many of the more rewarding ones. After all, modern Britain and modern India had been growing up alongside each other for a considerable time; many Indians had received practice enough in the methods of western economy; but the Burmans needed schooling in these methods. The missionaries brought schools of western stamp to Burma; but it was chiefly the simple Karens, not the Burmans, who sent their children to the mission schools. The Burmans remained loyal to their Buddhist monasteries which offered an education which was, indeed, good—good for the way of life which western economy was disrupting.

Disruption is the major theme of this history. A society which had been based on personal authority operating within the circle of custom has been eaten away by acquisitive individualism operating under an impersonal rule of law. In the village, old ways of getting a living disappear and so do the old values and habits. By way of illustration I shall mention a common-place habit. In former days the village had no sanitary problem; there was a special patch of bush in which the villagers used to wander as they felt the need. Market demand gives the patch of bush a commercial value and shrewd individuals divide it between them. The appearance of the village and its smell begins to shock European administrators. Fortunately, there is a modern State and it knows how to set matters right. The villagers have a latrine built for them ... They did not ask for it and they do not use it ... Our extensive and expensive paraphernalia of welfare services may be an irrelevance in tropical society. 'Welfare', Mr Furnival states, 'consists essentially in harmony between the individual and his environment; the environment must allow him to obtain both what he knows he wants and also what he wants without being aware of it'.

Perhaps the Burmans will get what they want now that the machinery of State is responsible to their own national will? But what is this national will? Western economic forces have created in Burma a plurality of wills, a bundle of communities —Burmans, Karens, Europeans, Indians, Chinese— each of which is internally eroded by economic individualism, each of which is tied to its neighbour by the cash nexus alone. How can Burma, which we have changed from an organic society into an organised business concern, find a unity of will and fashion itself into a Commonwealth?

I have reported Mr Furnival's historical argument; but this does not mean that I accept it all. On the political side, I feel that he puts too much blame upon the West, which did not invent all the cultural antipathies of Burma's plural society: for example, it would be untrue to say that Burmans and Karens loved each other until the British came. On the economic side, I find his statistical apparatus rather primitive. He examines no household budgets. He ignores the recent applications of balance of payments analysis to colonial economies.[1] He says roundly that national income accountancy would serve no useful purpose in a plural society such as Burma. Tell that to Miss Phyllis Deane![2] . . . All the same, his testimony about economic and social conditions in the Irrawaddy delta and about the tensions which everywhere pervade Burmese society has an authentic ring. Something has gone wrong in Burma.

It will help us to find out what this something is if we turn to the great success story of the Far East. In Japan, the optimistic logic of Smithian economics seems at first sight to justify itself fully.[3] Japan repeated the western miracle of combining a phenomenal increase of population with rising standards of living: between 1873 and 1940 her people increased from 35 millions to 73 millions, and in the early decades of this century her index of real wages almost doubled. The economic mechanisms of this

[1] Cf. *Balance of Payments of Nigeria in* 1936 by Penelope A. Bower (Basil Blackwood 1949).

[2] See *The Measurement of Colonial National Incomes,* by Phyllis Deane. (National Institute of Economic and Social Research, C.U.P. 1949).

[3] I follow G. C. Allen, *A Short Economic History of Modern Japan* (Allen & Unwin, 1948).

achievement are similar in principle to those we saw operating in Tasmania, though the scale of their operation is immensely greater. They can be quickly recognised in the statistical tables of trade, production and finance. Trade grew immensely when Japan opened her doors to western business; it began with a passive balance, but during the First World War it achieved an active one; it was based at the outset on the exchange of raw products for manufactures, but by 1914 nearly one third of Japanese exports, and by 1930 nearly one half of them, were finished manufactures. The figures of employment and production made the trade statistics intelligible; they revealed the familiar processes of transfer from country to town (though even today half the Japanese people remain country-dwellers) and from primary to secondary and tertiary occupations; they revealed also a great expansion of productivity and the rise of powerful new industries—textiles from the beginning of this century, heavy industries during the nineteen-thirties. The figures of finance showed that domestic accumulation of capital played the major part in the Japanese achievement: although external borrowing was considerable in the decade after the Russo-Japanese war, the trend of capital movements was reversed during the First World War and foreign debt became thereafter a steadily diminishing proportion of the country's total debt.

When we look beneath the mechanisms of this achievement for its historical explanations, we find that the Japanese enjoyed some good luck. For example, silkworm disease in Europe helped them in their first assault upon foreign markets; the falling price of silver in the 1880's helped them to make their dangerously inflated currency convertible; China's war indemnity helped them in the 1890's to move quietly from the silver standard to the gold standard. All the same, their good luck is only a small thing in comparison with their good management. The supreme manager was their own State. It was the State that swept away feudal and guild privileges and established an unfettered mobility of persons and goods. It was the State that educated its subjects in the new economic ways; it imported technicians from Europe; it sent people of its own to Europe to study the most modern industrial and commercial methods; it founded colleges and institutes for the study and diffusion of these methods at home. It was once again the State that promoted the new economic enterprises and in the early days managed them: it built and ran the railways, it bought ships and ran them, it established ship-building yards, it built and operated cotton mills, tile works, iron works, cement works: indeed, as Professor G. C. Allen has said, 'There was scarcely any important Japanese industry of Western type during the later decades of the nineteenth century that did not owe its establishment to State initiative'. Later, it is true, the State surrendered many of these enterprises to private capitalists; but these capitalists depended for their financial backing upon the banking system which the State established to gather in the savings of its subjects and mobilise them in support of export trade, agricultural expansion and industrial development.

Here then is the first explanation of the the contrast between Burmese and Japanese economic fortunes. In Burma, private enterprise—which in the largest and most modern ventures meant foreign enterprise—enjoyed unfettered opportunity under the protection of the State; in Japan, the State controlled private enterprise and was itself the chief enterpriser. It could not, however, have played its dominant part in economic change had it not been a national State and a strong one. States of this character cannot easily be made. The Japanese state grew from deep and strong roots in the national society.

Moreover, Japanese society was ready for direct participation in an economy of western type. Whereas in Burma the earlier growth of society had been ill adapted, except perhaps at the peasant level, to meet the impending impact of Western business, in Japan the earlier traditions and practices of the people were able to express themselves in the new forms of economic organisation. The Japanese were prepared for economic westernisation before it was thrust upon them. Their first great exporting industry, that of silk, retained its peasant foundations, which were strengthened rather than weakened when modern reeling mills and power-driven filiatures offered factory employment to the peasants' daughters. The cotton mills were altogether new; but they too depended for their labour supply upon the peasant families and they carried into the new age labour customs from the workshops of old Japan—a code of paternalistic practice under which employers fed and clothed and even entertained their workers, paid them bonuses at festive seasons and discharge allowances when they left the factory. It would be an exaggeration to say that Japanese labour did not have to face the same problems of adaptation as other industrialising countries had faced; but there is at least no reason to believe that these problems were more difficult in Japan than they had been in England a century earlier. Nor was the adaptation of capital more difficult in Japan. Its processes were in some respects dissimilar from European ones, but they were in tune with the Japanese past: the *zaibatsu*—family firms such as the Mitsui, the Mitsubishi, the Yasuda—were not a new creation of the western economy; they were already deeply rooted in the old order of Japanese life and found in the new order enlarged opportunities of wealth and power. It became their function to mobilise for industrial and commercial progress the savings which the State collected through its banking system. By contrast, there existed in Burma no national banking system and no native class of enterprising capitalists. The savings of prosperous Burmans went most conspicuously into the building of pagodas—an investment in Nirvana.

Let me now try to pull the threads together. My historical examples have revealed no new truths but they may help us to hold in due balance a number of familiar truths. First, there are some teachings of old-fashioned economics which the apostles of colonial development and welfare will ignore at their peril: a society which cannot by its own savings finance the progress it desires must strive to make itself credit-worthy and is most likely to succeed if it follows market opportunity along the path of comparative costs. Because its future prospects depend so much on present imports, it must look about for profitable export industries; it must also offer prospects of gain to people of enterprise—to its own people so far as possible, but if need be to foreigners also. It is better to have 'palm oil ruffians' to pioneer a thriving commerce than to have no economic pioneers at all.

This is pure Adam Smith, but I do not apologise for that; I find myself in the company of Joseph Schumpeter, who, having explained to his readers the futility of Lenin's *Imperialism* as a guide to imperial history, advised them to try the *Wealth of Nations* instead.[1] However, Schumpeter did not suggest that a book written in the eighteenth century was by itself a sufficient guide to twentieth century problems, or, for that matter, to the history of the nineteenth century. The palm oil ruffians, if left to themselves, do some bad things and leave many good things undone; if we in Europe think State action necessary to provide a groundwork for our economic system, to sustain its action in times of recession and to mitigate the class inequalities that it creates, how much more necessary is this action in countries where money income and public revenue fluctuate violently with the prices of a few exports, where the social fabric is extremely vulnerable to individualistic aggressions and where so many of the public services which we take for granted are lacking? I made this point by emphasising the contrast between Burma and Japan and I might have made it by carrying my Tasmanian story further; for democracy and the railways, which came to Australia together in the 'fifties, led immediately and inevitably to a wide extension of the functions of government. Indeed, countries which have a great deal of developmental work in front of them need an extra dose of State action. Unfortunately, this action

[1] *Capitalism, Socialism and Democracy*, by Joseph A. Schumpeter (2nd edition, New York 1947) p. 54.

40

presupposes a strong and uncorrupt State. Many of 'the under-developed countries' in the Far East and the Middle East and Africa do not as yet possess such a State nor the society on which it can be built. That is one of the reasons why they remain under-developed.

Today, in our colonial policies, we put upon the State as much as it can bear and sometimes more: in consequence, our applied economics, rigorous though they may be and should be in their techniques, are transmuted into political economy. But political economy makes little sense in colonial studies unless it is also social economy. That is the third lesson to be drawn from my historical examples. There may be uniformities in the economic behaviour of mankind but there are also peculiarities of economic behaviour within particular societies. We should think a good deal less about the 'natural propensity of mankind' and a good deal more about the historically-determined propensities of individual cultures. The Tasmanian aborigines, when they felt the impact of Western economic forces, showed no propensity at all except to die out or get themselves exterminated. The Red Indians of Canada showed a marked propensity to exchange beaver skins for kettles, firearms and rum; they acquired by trade fragments of western technology which increased their mobility, *élan* and destructiveness as hunters; they followed the chase westwards across the continent.

But when they had finished off the beaver they were finished themselves: at any rate, their old way of life was finished, and they had as yet hardly begun the slow and difficult task of learning a new way. At the other end of the scale we may study the amazing adaptation of Japanese society to the requirements and opportunities of western economy. But Japanese experience is exceptional. Whereas in some parts of Asia the peasants have made a quick response to widening markets and have sometimes proved themselves both tougher and more flexible than European planters, Asiatic labour, capital and enterprise have very often been slow in adapting themselves to the requirements of modern production. What is true of Asia is truer still of Africa, where the level from which change has to be made is so much lower. When I try to assess the speed with which a West African middle class may be expected to achieve real and enduring power, I observe not only its political but its economic behaviour. What does it do with its savings?

Expanding Europe has brought to Asia and Africa new opportunities but also new dangers. By bringing other peoples into our economy we have offered them the hope of release from the poverty of their ancient ways; but we have also corroded the values of their ancient ways. We hope that they will carry into a more spacious future much that has been good in their own past; but to achieve this synthesis they need time. Too often, we have given them too little time. Today, they are unwilling to give much time to themselves. Partly by intention and partly by accident we have been creating new classes whose leaders nowadays are in a hurry.

Towards what end are they hurrying? Political advancement is their most vehement claim. We should not find this claim unexpected or unwelcome: since Lord Durham's time, to go no further back, political advancement has been the guiding principle of our evolving Commonwealth. It has carried many British colonies to the status of unfettered national sovereignty. However, it would not have done so had it not been accompanied and sustained by economic advancement. There are many success stories which illustrate this truth. But there are also many failure stories which show the dangers that threaten a country—be it sovereign state or dependency—when its politicians are ardent but its peasants inert.

II

On the eve of the war a good many people were calling for vigorous State action to promote colonial development and welfare. I was one of them. Today, the policy I favoured then no longer needs advocates. It has become the new orthodoxy. In the past month or two I have been trying to take stock of it.

Let me first recall the changes that have occurred, during the past two decades, in trade policy and in the facts with which trade policy must reckon. Adam Smith guided British statesmen far into the nineteenth century and even into the twentieth; but he no longer guides them today. His theory, as List said, was 'cosmopolitical'; he combatted the economics of sovereignty and looked towards a well-ordered world in which the spontaneous trading partnerships of individuals would draw complementary regions into a unity. By an accident of history, Great Britain was able in the nineteenth century to make herself the metropolis of such an economy. Sterling freely convertible into gold or any foreign currency became international money. A market for long-term capital grew up alongside the discount market. Markets for every commodity became, under free trade, perpetually open. Merchant ships of all nations sailed all the oceans in the shelter of British naval power. Great Britain made herself the lender of last resort, the buyer of last resort, the policeman of last resort.

A few generations back all this looked permanent; but now we know how ephemeral it was. The drift of doctrine, in the new countries no less than in the old and even in Britain's own colonies, was away from the cosmopolitical system of economics to the national system. In our own time the drift has come to flood in Great Britain herself. There, doctrine moved with the facts. The British economy was waning in relative strength and other national economies were waxing; the time was coming when British resources would no longer be a sufficient prop of the world economy; no other nation and no combination of nations came forward as a new prop. So the world economy began to founder and Britain, like all the other nations, took to her own lifeboat. It was a lifeboat of imperial design, named the *Ottawa*. Many people hailed its launching with delight. But what would Sir Eyre Crowe have said about it? The much-vaunted harmonisation of British and world trading interests appeared unplausible now that Britain was the centre of a discriminating trade system; foreign nations found new causes, or at least new excuses, for their envy of the Empire's great possessions. Inside the Empire, tensions reminiscent of the eighteenth century began to make themselves felt again; some communities or some interests within these communities obtained the benefits of imperial preference; others carried the burdens, or complained that they were doing so. Broadly speaking, people in the Dominions were on balance favourable to the new order of preferences and quotas—as well might they be, seeing that they had been striving for half a century or more to convert Great Britain to their own protectionist philosophy; but people in the Colonies—excepting always the specially favoured sugar and tobacco colonies—believed that dearer imports were too high a price to pay for shelter in the imperial market, even when that shelter was not a mere fiction.[1]

I am, for the moment, discussing what people felt and said—not the economics of imperial trade, but its politics. They became a matter of international debate. The new course of British trade policy particularly displeased the Americans, who about this time were becoming tardy converts to the gospel of Adam Smith—for other peoples' commerce, if not always for their own. During the war and at its

[1] Imperial Preference could not ordinarily give effective shelter to commodities such as cocoa, oil seeds and rubber, whose supply within the Empire exceeded the Empire's demand. For a comparative analysis see *British Colonies in World Trade*, by F. W. Meyer (O.U.P. 1948).

close, Great Britain endorsed, with some reservations on the score of time and circumstance, the American principle of non-discriminating trade. As we all know, the impediments to this principle have proved far more intractable than the governments foresaw when they were negotiating the Mutual Aid Agreement and the American Loan. During the past five years, Great Britain and the sterling area have been entangled in a very different system. What has this meant for the colonies?

As importers, the colonies since the war have been much more closely tied to British suppliers than they were even in the post-Ottawa days of preferences and import quotas. Necessity, not deliberate imperial choice, has been the cause of this. German and Japanese manufacturers have been unable to compete in colonial markets and the same has been true in large measure of Indian manufacturers who, during the post-Ottawa years, were in certain lines the chief beneficiaries of imperial preference. American producers would have been able to compete powerfully over a wide range of goods had not scarcity of hard currency made the colonial demand ineffective. Dollar ceilings, instituted after the convertibility crisis of 1947, have had the effect of a stiff quota system against imports from America. As I suggested just now, nobody wanted these dollar ceilings but there was no escaping them if the reserves of the sterling area were to be saved. By consulting with colonial Governments London has done its best to mitigate the hardships that have fallen upon the colonial peoples. All the same, these hardships have been considerable and so have been their political repercussions. British supplies of capital and consumer goods have fallen far short of colonial demand; in consequence, the colonies have suffered very troublesome inflations. Moreover, British prices have sometimes been appreciably higher than American prices. In the early months of 1949 loud complaints came from the West Indies that they were being compelled to pay dear for inadequate British deliveries of all sorts of things that the Americans could offer plentifully and cheaply—textiles and tools, food stuffs, electrical goods, building materials and a long list of miscellaneous products. Is not this the famous exploitation? If it is, the British have been exploiting themselves just as harshly; for by the same dollar ceilings they have prevented themselves from procuring many plentiful and cheap goods that they badly want. Among other things, they have been paying dear for West Indian sugar, when they might, if only they had had the dollars, have bought more of their sugar more cheaply from Cuba. This line of thought may perhaps assuage our misgivings as moralists; but does it not excite our misgivings as economists? Is the British Commonwealth now becoming His Majesty's Association of High Cost Producers? Devaluation, it may be said, will get the costs of Commonwealth producers into line with American costs. Perhaps it will, but not necessarily in such a way as to bring to the people of the West Indies the plentiful and cheap goods they want, but cannot demand. Shall we, then, maintain the Commonwealth as His Majesty's Association of Rather Poor People? That way, we may make it an association that some people will want to get out of—though to be sure there may exist no better place, indeed no other place at all for them to get into, even if they belong (as the West Indies do not) to the Commonwealth's small minority of net dollar earners.

I do not see, given the situation the British found themselves in after the war, that their policy with regard to colonial imports could have been much different from what it has been. All the same, it would be dangerous to assume that the policy will automatically become more liberal as the situation grows easier. From the political point of view the situation may not be easier when managers and workers in British constituencies realise that excess capacity in the European steel industry has succeeded the seller's market. And what will Lancashire say when Asiatic mills become able again to export large quantities of textiles at fiercely competitive prices? Currency and exchange controls have not in fact been used to restrict colonial imports from soft currency areas; but up to the present there has been no temptation so to use them. That temptation may become very strong if German steel and Japanese piece goods are offered in colonial markets at prices which Britain cannot match; we may then see missionaries of full employment transformed into crusaders of imperial preference. Such an alliance might offer certain advantages; but it would also impose costs, and one can easily envisage ways in which an unfair proportion of the costs might be piled upon colonial consumers. I am not making a prophesy but I am sounding a warning. It seems highly improbable that the open door policy can ever return in its nineteenth century dress; but we must find ways and means of safeguarding what was permanently valuable in that policy. The colonial peoples are poor; we should prove ourselves unjust stewards if we allowed ourselves to drift into a trade policy which in its net effect was an incubus upon their earning power and standards of living.

I turn now to the situation of the colonies as exporters. Here too it is difficult to separate the short-term jerks from the long-term trends of change. Free access to world markets, which the theorists of the Dual Mandate prized as highly as they did the open door for imports, inevitably disappeared with the war. Its disappearance might have been thought a loss had it occurred in the era of buoyant prices when Lugard was systematising the liberal conception of trusteeship; but it could hardly have seemed a loss to colonial producers who had endured the price catastrophes of the 1930's. What the world market had meant in practice to a West African cocoa grower was the hard compulsion to sell his crop, at an unpredictable and sometimes a disastrous price, to a pan buyer or some other middle-man financed by one of the European firms. The firms were few and large and from time to time they joined each other in a buyers' ring; the producers were very many, very weak and completely unorganised. The war changed all this. The Ministry of Food made itself the sole buyer of the cocoa crop; it made the trading firms its buying agents; through them it offered the peasant a fixed, unfluctuating price. In the circumstances of the early war years, when short-term anxieties about shipping were combined with fears of excessive 'export surpluses' in long-term, nobody could allege that the price was an unfair one. The outlook began to change round about 1943, when British experts—though not at first supported by their American colleagues—began to forecast for the post-war years serious shortages at the sources of supply of food stuffs and most raw materials. In an era of shortages, bulk buying by an imperial government may become primarily an instrument for safeguarding consumer interests in the metropolitan country; colonial producers, or the journalists and politicians who write and speak on their behalf, may declare themselves exploited and raise a clamour for the world price. Actually, when the Ministry of Food and the Colonial Office start arguing with each other about the price to be paid for colonial sugar or oilseeds or tobacco, I personally cannot feel sure that the British consumer will get the benefit of the deal. Nor do I know, in these chaotic after-war conditions which have not even yet tidied themselves up, what precisely the world price is, or whether it exists. Consider the oils and fats. Since the war ended, their prices have been separate and sometimes divergent in the United Kingdom and United States, while buyers belonging to neither market have paid particularly high prices for the small quantities that have come their way. It would be fallacious to identify any of these separate transactions with the world market that used once to exist. There is, for example, a very different mixture of specific animal and vegetable products in British and American supplies; moreover, the Americans buy chiefly from producers within their own country, while the British buy chiefly from overseas producers. American prices have fluctuated sharply since the wartime controls were removed; at their peaks, in the early months of 1947 and again of 1948, they were much above the British level; but the decline which began in the summer of 1948 brought them back, seven or eight months later, to the controlled level of 1945. In contrast,

British prices followed a steady upward trend from 1945 to 1949; in the first half of 1949 they were from two to three times higher than at the end of the war. I have brooded over the monthly price quotations for oils and fats through these post-war years and find myself quite unable to reach any general conclusion about market price, let alone *pretium justum*. One thing I feel sure about: if any useful generalisation is to be made on this subject, it can only be made by induction, based upon detailed studies of particular commodities.[1]

Here it seems more useful to emphasise the large changes that have occurred, during and since the war, in the price-determining process. Little is now left of the system that I saw in West Africa ten years ago, under which a medley of unorganised producers faced a few highly organised firms. Nowadays, the typical contract is made between the Ministry of Food and a Statutory Board broadly representing the producers' interests.[2] The Produce Marketing Board of Sierra Leone, for example, is composed of three expert members nominated by the Governor, three producers' representatives nominated by the

[1] I have to thank Messrs Unilevers Ltd. for giving me detailed monthly figures of the price movements of oils and fats in the British and American markets since the war.

[2] The principles governing the United Kingdom's marketing policy for colonial products were stated by Sir Stafford Cripps on 17.9.48. See *Hansard*, Vol. 465, No. 14, Col. 1-4. In 1949-50 a tendency showed itself to narrow the area of bulk purchase; tin, timber, hides, sago flour, oranges and grapefruit reverted to private buying.

Assembly, and one representative of the Sierra Leone African Chamber of Commerce. I have no time to trace the steps by which this new order has come into existence nor to describe the variations which exist between different colonies and sometimes between different commodities within the same colony; it is the general effects of the change that need to be stressed. I shan't discuss the economic profit and loss of bulk-buying from this country's point of view; but there is one political effect that fills me with some apprehension. Bulk purchase of our daily bread and jam by a government department brings us, so to speak, right into the constituencies both of dominions and colonies. Politicians in the Australian wheatlands and the West Indian sugar islands, when their constituents are disappointed by a contract of purchase, now curse the British Government. It would be healthier for Commonwealth relations if they were still flinging their curses at bad businesss men or the market mechanism. However, if bulk purchase has this political disadvantage for us, bulk sale has a definite economic advantage for them. Colonial producers cannot hope to insulate themselves in long-term from world trends of commodity prices, (once again it is American demand which chiefly determines the price levels of copper and tin, coffee and cocoa and rubber), but the new order does offer them a release from the curse of sudden fluctuations. Their governments and marketing boards have learned the trick that the New Zealanders were practising before the war—to put something into the kitty in the years of good prices so as to hold the producer's reward at a stable level when the price falls. In many British colonies, accumulated commodity profits that were in part withheld from the growers during recent years have served some other important functions; in short term, they have mitigated the evils that arise from too much money chasing too few goods: in long term, they are an investment fund that can be employed in the rehabilitation and expansion of existing industries, or the development of new ones.

Development—it is time to introduce this theme, now the dominating one in discussions of colonial policy. The Development and Welfare policy began to be born when the idealists of colonial trusteeship dissolved their time-hallowed partnership with the individualists and made a new one with the planners. Its legislative landmarks are years of crisis: 1929, the 'economic blizzard'; 1940, *annus mirabilis* of national valour; 1945, year of victory; 1947, crisis of convertibility. I have read the *Hansards* in the hope of recapturing the tone of discussion in these years. One thing that has impressed me in my reading is the fluctuation of emphasis with which the purposes of colonial development have been stated. In 1929, when the first small act was passed, the accent fell heavily upon Great Britain's needs; in the ardent years of 1940 and 1945 it fell almost exclusively upon colonial needs; in 1947, when the Colonial Development Corporation and Overseas Food Corporation were set up, it fell upon the reciprocal and interlocking interests of Britain and the colonies. Although there may be some awkwardness in piping down from the lofty tone of pure altruism,[1] the last note pleases me most; in the era of planning, as in the era of individualism, British democracy will more readily persevere in its colonial duty if its benevolent aspirations are tempered by some alloy of economic realism.

Amidst the variations of emphasis that may be detected in the discussions of the past ten years one note has been constant—the note of great expectations. It is commonly pitched high in times of great endeavour: I recall those ardent imperial developers who, at the end of the First World War, glorified the dazzling wealth of British West Africa—wealth enough to pay off the entire British war debt and endow British Trade Unionists with a six hour working day![2] This time, the propaganda has been

[1] E.g. In the annual report on *The Colonial Empire*, 1947-8, it was thought fit to say (Cind. 7433, para. 11) that the heightened emphasis on metropolitan, as distinct from colonial interests, following the convertibility crisis, signified a return to the dual mandate—to promote the interests not only of the colonial peoples but 'all mankind'. But it is un-historical to speak of the dual mandate outside the context of liberal trade policy and the 'open door'.

[2] See *Survey of British Commonwealth Affairs*, by W. K. Hancock, Vol. II, Part 1, pp. 107-8.

less exuberant; but, even so, it has exaggerated both the input that can be spared for colonial development and the output that can be expected.

Since 1947, it has become usual to estimate the output against the background of our balance of payments preoccupations. How many dollars will the Colonial Development policy earn for the sterling area? How many dollars will it save? At the end of the war there was a net drain from the Colonial Empire; but by 1948 an appreciable net gain had been achieved.[1] However, it was the gain of a few commodities only—rubber, cocoa, tin— and of the two or three colonies that produced these commodities; moreover, it began rapidly to vanish when American prices fell in the first half of 1949. Obviously, the dollar gain from these commodities possesses a chancy element, despite the recent recovery following devaluation and the strong renewal of American demand. The contribution of British colonies to United Kingdom imports has shown a steadier rate of climb—from a little over 5 per cent of the total in 1938 to approximately 10 per cent in 1949. However, we must remember that the volume of British imports is lower than it was before the war, while the increased colonial contribution to this

[1] The net gain in American and Canadian dollars for 1948 was the equivalent of £14 million (before devaluation), made up of a £6 million deficit with U.S.A. and a £20 million positive balance with Canada. See *A Review of Commonwealth Trade*, H.M.S.O. 1949, pp. 8–9 (33rd Report of Commonwealth Economic Committee).

smaller total has been secured in part by switching from foreign markets to the British market. The index of volume based upon the chief exports from the Colonial Empire shows an encouraging, but not an exciting rise: with the base at 100 in 1946, the figure is 119 for 1936 and 149 for 1948: the estimate for 1950-3, or perhaps we should say the target, is 184.[1] Neither the official record of past performance nor the official guesses at future performance justify popular hopes that the colonies of Britain or those of all the European powers together can quickly be made a bountiful larder for the British people or for the whole Marshall Aid group of countries. The calculations of O.E.E.C., of the economists of U.N.O.,[2] and expert bodies in this country such as the Colonial Primary Products Committee all emphasise the same truth: in short term no sensational increase in production can be expected; in long term the increase may well be very important, provided there is sufficient investment in colonial development.

But here comes the rub: it is now quite clear that the expectations of input into colonial development

[1] See Cmd. 7958, para. 233. These index numbers are a later and slightly revised edition of those given in Cmd. 7715, para. 239. The level of performance in different parts of the Empire is uneven: for example, it is doubtful whether British West Africa has up to the present made any marked contribution to the rise in the index of volume.

[2] The problem is clearly discussed in *Economic Survey of Europe* 1948 (United Nations Department of Economic Affairs) Ch. 8. See especially Table 102.

were pitched far too high during the war and after its close. In reading the *Hansards* I noticed one gap that in retrospect seems scarcely credible: balance of payments difficulties received not a single mention in the colonial debates of 1945. In that year, nearly everybody under-rated the competing claims that would be made upon the nation's diminished store of resources.

Some of these claims may be stated in strictly economic terms: what, for example, is the estimate of comparative return upon investments in food production directed to Northern Australia, or—what is perhaps more promising—to the settled farmlands of the Australian east and south? or to Tanganyika? or to West Africa? or to British agriculture? or—assuming that we are willing to think less imperially—to continental Europe? These questions are not easy to answer and I am not aware that anybody has tried very hard to answer them. Politics force their way into the investigation and complicate the assessment of competing claims upon our scarce resources of capital. To take one example: other countries—let us say Australia—may be set on an investment course very different from the one that would best suit British needs. To take another example: it is necessary to direct overseas investments with some regard to the needs of those countries that are, so to speak, in the front line of Western defence against Soviet attack. Consider for a moment the nine Far Eastern countries contained within the triangle Afghanistan, Indonesia, Indo-China: those of them that remain within the British Commonwealth, either as sovereign states or as colonial dependencies, are on the average distinctly more prosperous than their neighbours; but the area is one strategical whole and a prominent article of western strategy is economic—to win the race between economic progress and population increase in a region which already holds about half the world's people. The statesmen of the Commonwealth have recently been making speeches on this theme at the Colombo Conference; but I do not know whether they have worked out a realistic five-year or ten-year plan. If they have, I feel sure that its figures are quite frightening and that they make no sense at all unless the United States speedily and in a very big way goes into action on President Truman's Fourth Point.[1] So far, there has come from the United States much talk about the Fourth Point but not much action. Meanwhile, Great Britain herself has been undertaking quite a lot of

[1] The Fourth Point is often referred to, but its precise content is seldom stated. In his Inaugural Address of 20th January 1948, President Truman said that American scientific and industrial resources would be made available to under-developed countries; but he added the following qualifications: that American resources were not unlimited; that the chief American aim would be to help the peoples concerned to improve their conditions by their own efforts; that other nations would be called upon to co-operate, especially through the special agencies of U.N.O.; that American business, private capital, agriculture and labour should

fourth pointery—Mr Bevin at the Colombo Conference estimated its total value at £750 millions—
through rehabilitation and development in Hong
Kong, Malaya and Borneo, through financial aid to
Burma, above all through the release of sterling
balances to India and Pakistan. Some of this work
falls within the framework of the colonial development policy, but not the greater part of it; its net
effect has been to push colonial claimants to a lower
place in the queue.

Indeed, when we consider the arithmetic of
colonial development since the war we can hardly
escape a feeling of anti-climax. To begin with, the
targets of investment have not in fact been set nearly
so high as most people seem to think. I have tried
to make a rough guess at the money total of our
plans, or perhaps I should say our hopes. Adding up
the monies of the development and welfare fund, of
the two big corporations, of the loans that colonial
governments plan to raise and the sums that private
business-men may hope to invest, the total that I
reach would represent for the period 1945-55 little

be brought in; that guarantees to investors must be balanced by
guarantees to the peoples concerned against exploitation.

Discussions following this pronouncement, which was promptly
welcomed by Mr Bevin, have explored possibilities of action through
E.C.A., through the Economic and Social Council of U.N.O. and its
Special Agencies such as the International Bank, and through private
investment. It should be noted that under the Fourth Point the rôle of
the British Commonwealth is that of contributor as well as
beneficiary.

more than £1 per head per annum for the population of the whole Colonial Empire. Of course, there are additional sources of finance for investment: taxation and the accumulated balances of good price years may make an important contribution: I have already mentioned the useful sums salted away by some of the export marketing boards. But you will observe that I am still speaking of what finance may permit and *not* of the physical investment actually achieved. It is well known that physical limitations, not financial ones, have been governing the pace of colonial development from the end of the war until very recently. Of £120 millions theoretically available under the act of 1945, only about £20 millions had been actually issued by the end of the financial year 1948-9 (or £25½ millions if we count back to the act of 1940). As for the accumulated sterling balances, they were still just about as high in 1949 as they were when the war ended—which means that the Colonial Empire, while receiving loans and grants of various kinds from the United Kingdom, has itself been granting reciprocal financial aid to the United Kingdom.[1] A lover of paradox might be moved to argue that the net investment of this country in its colonial dependencies from 1945 up to

[1] See Cmd. 7715, para 392 and Cmd. 7958, para. 468. At 31 December 1948, the sterling balances of the Colonial Empire totalled some £610 millions and during the following twelve months they increased slightly.

1949 was *nil*. The argument may be statistically plausible; but it is not the only truth nor the most relevant one. Sterling reserves in London, whether they belong to dominions or to colonies, serve a variety of essential functions; the New Zealand government knows that only a part of them can be drawn upon for capital development and the Nigerian government must accept similar limitations and indeed some additional ones.[1] While Great Britain has benefited from the proceeds of colonial exports left in London, she herself has helped the colonies by setting aside, quite separately, funds for their development. Admitting all this, I still believe that I have made an important point: the financing of colonial development, unlike the release of sterling balances to India or Pakistan, has not up to the present been a real strain upon British resources; nor have the colonies, with one or two exceptions, received the large inputs which the orators have encouraged them to expect.

Instead, they have suffered an acute shortage of the capital and consumer goods that they must have if the development and welfare policy is to be translated from rhetoric into substance. Fortunately, the worst time of shortage seems now to be past; whereas, for example, the colonies in the first three post-war years were receiving considerably less steel

[1] A detailed analysis of the various functions performed by sterling balances of colonial territories would be useful.

than before the war, they have since 1948 been receiving considerably more. All the same, British resources remain scanty compared with the many claims upon them, and are likely to be scantier still when the period of Marshall Aid ends. In the coming years, as in the past ones, some overpitched hopes will be disappointed. For example, there seems to me scant opportunity for extending the principle so ardently affirmed in the debates of 1940 and 1945, that colonial needs, as distinct from colonial capacities, should largely determine the allocation of resources. Comparative estimates of investment per head of population show that Nigeria—to take one example—stands very low in the list compared with the Gold Coast, Tanganyika and some other African colonies, not to mention colonies in the Far East. We have been directing the flow of capital according to our estimates—be they right or wrong —of the comparative return to be expected. Our socialist age, hardly less than its individualist predecessor, finds itself respecting the maxim: 'To those who have shall be given'.

The same criterion of economic capacity must in large measure govern the distribution of investment within a particular colony. I have not time to examine in any detail the complicated processes through which this criterion becomes effective in the actual practice of the colonial governments, the big corporations and the private business firms; but

I shall say just a little about 'outline planning'[1] by the Colonial Office—its attempt to sketch a comprehensive strategy for the economic development of specific colonial areas. The planners appear to be influenced increasingly by estimates of national (or territorial) income, output and expenditure. I know that doubts have been expressed about the wisdom of applying the methods of national income accountancy to economies which are in large measure non-monetary,[2] but I personally find them helpful. I find myself gaining from them a more vivid appreciation of the comparative magnitudes of economic activity within a specific colony, and its most likely growing points: so far from feeling myself fobbed off with monetary abstractions, I feel more powerfully impelled towards particular concrete enquiries—which are, indeed, the natural and necessary sequel of every attempt to construct an economic picture in the large.

Today I shall continue to look at things in the large. There are three general questions of colonial economic strategy, each much debated in recent years, upon which an historian may have something useful to say. The first concerns the rival claims of

[1] The Colonial Office, arguing that detailed planning from Whitehall was both undesirable and impossible, used this phrase in reply to criticism by the Select Committee on Estimates. See *1st Report of the Select Committee on Estimates*, Session 1948–9. App. 1.

[2] E.g. by Professor S. H. Frankel in the *Economic Journal*, Dec., 1949, p. 593, reviewing *The Measurement of Colonial National Incomes: an Experiment*, by Miss Phyllis Deane.

primary and secondary industry in development policy as a whole. The second concerns the rival claims of export production and home food supply in agricultural policy. The third raises in a new form the old controversy between the claims of peasant and plantation agriculture. Each of these problems is too often stated in a form which suggests that we must choose either the whole of this alternative or the whole of that; whereas, so it seems to me, the real need is quite often to find the particular mixture that best suits the circumstances of a particular territory.

To start with manufacturing industry: colonial nationalists are prone almost to idolise it, as if it offered a magic key to wealth and power. This most certainly it does not do—yet it is not enough merely to tell the nationalists that they are wrong and that agricultural progress is what they ought to want. Agricultural progress itself implies some measure of industrial progress as its consequence (you may recall my Tasmanian example) and sometimes even as its cause; for, where population is thick on the ground and the farm unit is very small, the growth of alternative employments in manufacture may be a necessary condition for the improvement of agricultural technique. There have been countries, such as eighteenth century England, where this parallel development of agriculture and industry has been achieved without purposeful action by the State; but in our own time State action can hardly be dispensed with. During the second half of the nineteenth century, self-governing colonies of European stock began to use the instrument[1] of tariff protection: in the tropical dependencies of to-day other means of State intervention may be more appropriate—for example, the establishment of trading estates, as advocated recently by Professor Arthur Lewis.[2] Whatever its mechanisms may be, the industrialising policy will impose costs upon communities whose standards of living are very low; but some price is worth paying in short-term in order to hasten the expansion and diversification of employment. Where the balance may best be struck between the advantages and the costs will vary with the special circumstances of particular territories. Can we, however, feel certain that the metropolitan country is willing to tackle the problem in each instance from the standpoint of the colony's interest? From the eighteenth century to the present day, a desire for manufacturing advance, interwoven very often with the desire for political advance, has been a recurrent aspiration of colonies; equally recurrent has been the disposition of manufacturing interests in the metropolitan country to oppose, or at least to

[1] One should not however underestimate the spontaneous movement of vigorous communities of primary producers along the industrial road nor forget the classic case of free-trade New South Wales, which kept pace with protectionist Victoria in manufacturing development.

[2] *Colonial Development* by W. Arthur Lewis: Manchester Statistical Society, January 1949.

belittle these colonial claims. During the nineteenth century, the success of British colonial policy—as witness the affair of the Canadian tariff in 1859—was due in great part to the Government's determination, tardy though it may at times have been, to resist the pressure of particular interests at home when they attempted to restrict colonial autonomy. But in the planned economy of to-day the government no longer stands above industry; government and particular interests are sometimes the same voice. I have seen no sign as yet of the voice becoming harsh in the disastrous eighteenth-century way: up to the present the indications are quite different. All the same, we should be on our guard against the temptations that may assail a democratised imperium which holds in its hands both political sovereignty and direct economic control, or even proprietorship.

So much for the industrial front of colonial policy. It has considerable economic importance and still greater psychological and political importance. Nevertheless, it is not the main front. If there is genuine agricultural progress in the colonies we may take it for granted there will be some industrial progress too; the question is merely how much and how soon; but if there is no agricultural progress, or not enough of it, we may expect in most colonies nothing but ruin, ruin of the land and ruin of the population whose increase outstrips returns from the land—as in some areas it already does. Consequently, even if we were tempted to give manufacturing efficiency the first place in our endeavours, we should soon find ourselves forced to recognise the primacy of agriculture. Agricultural backwardness may itself be the root cause of a poor industrial performance. It has, for example, been suggested recently that 'malignant malnutrition' is one of the causes of the low efficiency of railway workers in Kenya:[1] if this be true, the cure must be sought where the disease originates— in the malnutrition of African mothers. It must be sought through a new way of life upon the land.

Nutrition studies have considerably reinforced a disposition, which has become fairly prevalent during recent decades, to insist that the primary function of the land is to produce food for the people that live upon it. Does this mean that the production of export crops has to be sacrificed? The problem is often stated in the *either . . . or* form; but this may be distortion, since export production may itself be the condition of improving production to meet home needs. For example, the tenant families of the Gezira are winning from their forty-acre holdings an average cash profit of over £50 per annum and they have achieved this success by following a prescribed agricultural rotation in which there is always the following distribution of land: cotton,

---

[1] *African Labour Efficiency Survey*, ed. C. H. Northcote. (Colonial Publications No. 3) pp. 84-93 *Medical Aspects of Inefficiency*, by H. C. Trowell.

10 acres; guinea corn, 5 acres; lubia (a forage crop), 5 acres; fallow 20 acres. In this agricultural scheme the food needs of the cultivators are provided for and so are the needs of the land; but it is cotton, the export crop, that has created the high peasant incomes and the food supplies and the soil conserving rotation and, indeed, the whole community; were it not for cotton the Gezira would still be desert. Here we see a new instance of the same truth that was prominent in my last lecture: an undeveloped country whose people intend to better their condition must find a profitable export trade, which will almost certainly be based, in the beginning at any rate, upon primary production. Even great manufacturing countries such as America and Japan and, for that matter, England, once began their journey towards wealth and power along this road. The need of undeveloped countries for export staples is so fundamental that some communities have sometimes found it worth while to let others grow much of their food for them; the Maritime Provinces of Canada made themselves a decent living by concentrating their labour, capital and skill on fishing, saw milling, shipping and ship building, while they depended on American farmers for their daily bread; the colony of New South Wales, while it was building its fortunes on wool, depended similarly on Tasmanian and South Australian farmers. Or, to cite examples nearer to

71

us in time, the peoples of Ceylon and Malaya have been enjoying higher standards of living than their neighbours because their tea and rubber and tin have enabled them to procure the necessities of life at a much lower cost in labour and capital than a self-sufficient agriculture would have necessitated. Despite this, if Burma and Siam, as seems quite likely, have ceased to be reliable exporters of rice, both Ceylon and Malaya will each have to increase their investment in consumption crops. There are strategical uncertainties, there are payments difficulties, there are arguments of ecology or social health or economic prudence that can be advanced against overspecialised production for export; nobody now denies that cash crop farming should, wherever possible, be reinforced by an agricultural practice that spreads the market risk and is besides geared to nutritional need and soil conservation. What we have to do is to use our commonsense and strike a balance between different advantages and costs. In doing so, we should take especial care to avoid getting the worst of both worlds, as has happened in many parts of Kenya, where cash crop farming has been adopted without inducing a corresponding change in the methods of primitive self-sufficiency. With this combination of evils, the dangers both to living standards and to the soil become claimant. Change there must be if disaster is to be staved off. But on what lines will it proceed and how will it be brought about?

Everybody agrees that African society, by and large (in a few exceptional areas good cultivation is established already) needs an agricultural revolution. One way of trying to start it is by launching 'a military operation'[1] against three million acres of fly-infested scrub, pouring in money by tens of millions of pounds, improvising the basic services, letting rip the bulldozers, equipping twenty thousand or more labourers with expensive plant and trusting that all this, somehow or other, will be an example to Kikuyu peasants on their small eroded plots. There is, however, another way, which I saw demonstrated, ten years ago, in the Reserves in Southern Rhodesia.[2] The Native Agricultural Department there had at that time an annual budget of not quite £13,000—as compared with £248,000 voted in the same year to European Agriculture. Its chief, Mr E. D. Alvord—I take pleasure in recalling his name—could not afford to purchase expensive contour-ridging equipment; so he improvised a ridging implement by putting together a railway sleeper and a gum pole: any native cultivator could do the same. He did not have money enough to run a demonstration farm; so he went through the

---

[1] *A Plan for the Mechanised Production of Groundnuts in East and Central Africa*, Cmd. 7030, Feb. 1947. The estimated labour requirement in the original plan was 25,000 labourers at the peak of clearing and 30,000 cultivators after the land was cleared.

[2] *Survey of British Commonwealth Affairs*, by W. K. Hancock, Vol. II, Part 2, pp. 107-8.

reserves and found interested peasants ('co-operators' he called them) who were willing to take his demonstrators on to their holdings. Now, I myself have never seen anybody except managers and employees on demonstration farms in Africa and I have wondered sometimes whether any African cultivators at all ever visit their marvels; but the cultivator is bound to take notice if a little manure and a simple crop rotation double the yield of mealies on his own holding. Perhaps it is harder to touch the springs of communal action; but Alvord improvised a simple kind of enclosure, without any expenditure upon fencing, by rearranging the village huts so that they separated the arable from the pasture. When I was with him, he showed me a waiting list of thirty or more reserves which were asking him to come and rearrange their agricultural pattern in this way. I believed that I was present at the beginnings of an agricultural revolution. Money certainly was not its motive force: £13,000 a year do not go very far. It was an achievement of missionary zeal, or mass education—you can choose last century's phrase or this century's, whichever pleases you. Here was a man who knew his job and knew his fellow men— the most important part of his job. He knew how to carry them along with him in creative change; he had brought them to the point where they were pulling upon the administration to get things done instead of sullenly resisting its push.

I dare say he would have done better work still if he had had more money: please don't think that I am against spending money in the colonies. What I am discussing is how to get value for money. Money signifies resources that are very scarce in this country —too scarce, I think, to justify a second super-scale plantation enterprise on the Tanganyika model. The motives behind plantation agriculture are to-day what they have always been—to develop production in quantities which seem too large and at a pace which seems too hot for peasant cultivators—but the methods are different nowadays from what they used to be. Land is still plentiful and cheap if one goes to the right places; but labour has become scarce; for it would be inconceivable now to re-introduce the indenture system, which last century was the source of supply for plantation labour. A plentiful supply of capital, therefore, must make good the scarcity of labour. The new plantation methods assume that Britain has a plethora of the factor of production which, as we all know, is in critical short supply. These methods are, in consequence, out of tune with the basic requirements of British economy.

But suppose that this were not so—suppose that we were our Victorian great-grandfathers, with a large surplus on our yearly balance of payments for investment overseas; or suppose that we were the Americans, looking along the Fourth Point road for ways of mitigating our embarrassments as a creditor nation—even then we should need to seek good value for money. By good value I mean economic return—it need not always be direct or immediate—and also human return. These two things hang closely together in the colonies; for economic progress demands rapid social change, which will get stuck unless the colonial societies themselves co-operate in the process of change. The high economic return I saw on a paltry investment in the Reserves of Southern Rhodesia was a dividend upon personal genius in eliciting human co-operation. Genius, you will say, is something we can't budget for: all the same many of our people have a dash of the kind I am talking about. Colonial governments should make the most of it.

I do not wish to seem one-sided. I am aware of the strong case that has frequently been made for the plantation system. In the past, it has been the means —sometimes the only means—of introducing those scientific methods of breeding, sowing, cultivating, harvesting, processing, that colonial territories so badly need. It has been a means of attracting capital, raising territorial income, increasing public revenue and thereby laying foundations for economic and social advance in the colonial society at large. Sometimes it has had an important educational impact upon colonial society; the peasants have imitated the planters and have even outmatched them in economic competition. Here I see a clue worth following: colonial attitudes being what they now are, it seems unwise to embark upon vast plantation enterprises in the hope that they *may* lead to peasant participation at some future time; rather should we seek peasant participation as an immediate and essential objective of policy. Responsible opinion in West Africa, mindful of mistakes made elsewhere, has already approved this policy.[1] It may seem slow in fulfilment; but slow beginnings and even procrastination are better than a Gadarene rush down a steep hill.

To insist upon the need for peasant participation does not mean opposition to mechanised agriculture. When a mission of experienced agriculturists affirms that Africans must take a leap from the hoe and cutlass age into the tractor age, it is not for me to dissent—though I may hope that, while some Africans are taking this leap, others will be moving quietly from the digging stick age to the hoe and cutlass age, while others still will be getting better

[1] See *Report of West African Oil Seeds Mission*, Col. No. 224, Nov. 1947. The Mission, while advocating certain projects of mechanised cultivation, insisted that they should be tried out initially in small pockets of unoccupied land, closely adjoining peasant populations which might be expected very soon to feel their educational impact. It also insisted that there should be a quick transition from paid labour to a participating peasantry. The Nigerian Government went further; they aimed at securing peasant participation from the very start and set about collecting relevant data in the Sudan. See *Land Usage in the Sudan in its relation to a Nigerian Mechanised Groundnut Scheme*. (Govt. Printer, Kaduna, 1949.)

hoes and cutlasses. We should always remember that large returns may be won from village cultivators—and why not also from village craftsmen?—with the expenditure of little money. But I agree that we must have tractors too, provided the cost accountants prove them a sound proposition; provided also that we find some way of making the African feel that they are for him, and not merely for us.[1]

Massive capitals and large projects there have to be—in research, transport, water conservation, swamp draining, mining, power plant, cement works. These massive enterprises are bound to seem remote from the ordinary African: even in England, we don't feel for the railways and the coal mines a thrill of ownership and participation . . . But neither do we think them foreign. It is this feeling of foreign-ness that has to be combatted in the colonies. May it not be effectively combatted if genuine self-government—which includes local government—advances in close step with the development policy? The new transport scheme may not seem so remote when local men of the District Development Council are called in to propose the feeder roads which will link village paths to the trunk system; even the peasants may feel that the scheme touches them when they find that it will free them from the

[1] In this connection special interest attaches to the current experiments in nutrition and mechanised agriculture in the Gambia.

exhausting and expensive curse of carrying heavy loads for long distances on the top of their heads. The same kind of response may be forthcoming when the District Development Council is called upon to make proposals for safeguarding its own forests and catchment areas, for conserving its water and soil, for developing crops and livestock and promoting industries and crafts. If a new mill is to be erected in the district for the processing of palm oil, some means may be found of vesting it in district ownership. If a tractor is to be brought into a village or a group of villages, a farmers' co-operative may be made its owner ... But these rosy visions assume that the colony possesses men who know how to get a co-operative started and how to keep it on the rails in the early difficult days, men who can understand the economic plans of headquarters and translate them imaginatively and realistically at the village level of requirements and capacities. Such men are scarce in comparison with the jobs that need doing. We talk a lot about our scarce resources and usually we mean that we have not got enough money to spare; but the men are scarcer than the money. We have not got enough men or rather we have failed to find them. A few weeks ago I read a first rate plan, an exciting plan, for developing a colony: indeed, I had this plan in my head when I spoke just now of jobs to be tackled. But how can this plan come to life when the colony, on its existing establishment—I say nothing of the increase that is needed—has one vacancy in every five? When it is short of administrators, teachers, doctors, geologists, engineers, agriculturalists— indeed everybody?

I have come to the end. It is not the end I expected when I started to prepare these papers and I dare say it is more humdrum than the end you have been expecting. You might have preferred me to discuss the recent United Nations reports on *Methods of Financing Economic Development in Under-Developed Countries*.[1] Indeed, I think these reports very helpful. For example, their insistence upon the importance of domestic accumulation and investment accords very closely with some of the historical experience I put before you in my first lecture: equally accept- able to me is their insistence that the stimulation and mobilisation of domestic savings is in large measure a problem of institutions and psychology. Again, the reports are very much to the point in their dis- cussion of capital imports: in particular, they bring into sharp relief the conflict of views, between potential lenders and would-be borrowers, about the conditions that justify large-scale transfers of capital. All this you might have wished me to dis- cuss. You might also have wished me to relate the

[1] Lake Success, 1949. The publication contains reports or statements by various International Agencies, introduced by a report of the Secretariat of the United Nations.

comparatively modest total of capital requirements in British colonies to the astronomical figures in which the experts of Lake Success portray the requirements of under-developed territories in the world at large.

Yes, I understand the fascination of the 'one world' approach. But I am by temperament the kind of person who likes to think that he will do some good to his neighbours, as well as to himself, if he makes a job of cultivating his own garden. If I were now preparing a third paper, I think I should make it still more provincial than these two have been. Above all, I should ask how are we to get the right men for the work and get enough of them. I do not know the answers but I have some notions of how to set about looking for them. They must be found. Our Commonwealth has a long history and some persons of a narrow political outlook assume—as they have done before—that it is approaching its close; but, if we take the true measure of human needs and dangers and opportunities in this age, we shall find ourselves summoned to make a new beginning.

For EU product safety concerns, contact us at Calle de José Abascal, 56–1°,
28003 Madrid, Spain or eugpsr@cambridge.org.

www.ingramcontent.com/pod-product-compliance
Ingram Content Group UK Ltd.
Pitfield, Milton Keynes, MK11 3LW, UK
UKHW042209180425
457623UK00011B/114